**SCHOLASTIC**

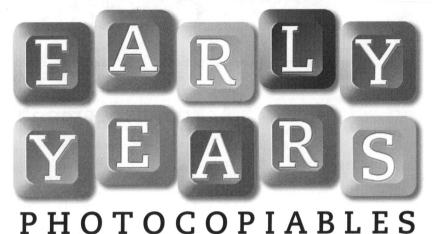

# PHOTOCOPIABLES

# ICT

## Aspects of Knowledge and Understanding of the World

# INCLUDES CD-ROM
# WITH OVER 100 ACTIVITIES

■ FAVOURITE THEMES ■
■ EARLY LEARNING GOALS ■ DIFFERENTIATED ACTIVITIES ■

Text © 2006 Scholastic Ltd

Designed using Adobe InDesign

Published by Scholastic Ltd
Villiers House
Clarendon Avenue
Leamington Spa
Warwickshire CV32 5PR

www.scholastic.co.uk

Printed by Bell & Bain

123456789  6789012345

**British Library Cataloguing-in-Publication Data**
A catalogue record for this book is available from the British Library.

ISBN 0-439-94489-9
ISBN 978-0439-94489-2

The rights of the authors of this work have been asserted by them in accordance with the Copyright, Designs and Patents Act 1988. Extracts from The National Literacy Strategy © Crown copyright. Reproduced under the terms of HMSO Guidance Note 8.

# Credits

**Series Editor**
Sally Gray

**Assistant Editor**
Jennifer Howard

**Series Designer**
Anna Oliwa

**Designer**
Erik Ivens

## Acknowledgements

The publishers gratefully acknowledge permission to reproduce the following copyright material:

**Text**
© **Suzanne Edwards:** Pairs, Heavier or lighter?, Play time!, Christmas stamps; © **Jean Evans:** Helping hands, Musical interlude; © **Anne Farr:** Weather centre, Cook it!, In the picture, It's for you, Write about…, What happened next?, Story time, Art gallery; © **Janice Filer:** Follow the tin robot, Yellow submarine; © **Sally Gray:** Play-writing, Photo fun!, What's on TV?, Tell a tale, The writing corner, Say the sound, Little red book, The paint shop, At the park, Walkie-talkies, Remote control, Make yourself at home, Talking books, Plug in and listen, CD favourites; © **Pauline Kenyon:** Musical maps; © **Barbara J Leach:** What's the difference?; © **Ann Montague-Smith:** Pattern allsorts; Dr Hannah Mortimer: Staying safe; © **Jenni Tavener:** Bubbles poem, There's a tiny caterpillar, The lost puppy, Our soup recipe, Water search, Hickory dickory dock, Decorating, Sandcastle flags; © **Brenda Williams:** When I went shopping; © **Irene Yates:** Invitation, Shopping list, What do you hear?, Make up the story, Super stories, Favourite books

**Illustrations**
© **Clare Boyce:** Musical maps; © **Terry Burton:** Helping hands, Musical interlude; © **Frances Cony:** Pairs; © **Kelly Dooley:** Christmas stamps; © **Lynne Farmer:** Sandcastle flags; © **Cathy Hughes:** Follow the tin robot, Yellow submarine, Bubbles poem, There's a tiny caterpillar, The lost puppy, Our soup recipe, Water search, Hickory dickory dock, Decorating, Staying safe; © **Jo Moore:** Little red book, The paint shop, At the park; © **Jan Nesbitt:** What's the difference?; © **Julia Oliver:** Heavier or lighter?, Play time!; © **Angie Sage:** Weather centre, Cook it!, In the pictures, It's for you, Write about …, What happened next?, Story time, Art gallery and Say the sound; © **Jessica Stockham:** When I went shopping, Walkie-talkies, Remote control, Make yourself at home, Talking books, Plug in and listen, CD favourites; © **Sami Sweeten:** Pattern allsorts; © **Jenny Tulip:** Invitation, Shopping list, What do you hear?, Make up the story, Super stories, Favourite books, Play-writing, Photo fun!, What's on TV?, Tell a tale, The writing corner.

Every effort has been made to trace copyright holders and the publishers apologise for any inadvertent omissions.
Visit our website at www.scholastic.co.uk

# Contents

# Introduction

This book forms part of a series of photocopiable activity books for the Early Years. The books and their accompanying CD-ROMs provide early years practitioners with a bank of lively, differentiated activities that focus on a particular skill or curriculum area. The chapters in each book are divided into popular themes.

The ideas in this book have been selected from previously published Scholastic early years series. They have been updated to meet new curriculum requirements and many have been differentiated, with alternative activity sheets for supporting and extending the work provided on the CD-ROM.

## Using this book

*Early Years Photocopiables – ICT* contains five chapters based on the popular themes of 'Let's play', 'Home and away', 'How things work', 'Stories and rhymes' and 'Creative fun'. Each chapter contains two pages of teacher's notes and ten photocopiable activity sheets. The activities are intended to be used to support work in aspects of Knowledge and Understanding of the World and may be used in any order to suit your own planning or to fit in with your current learning themes.

The photocopiable activity sheets can be used in a flexible manner – you may wish to use some of the activities for assessment and record-keeping purposes and many are suitable for sending home with the children.

Sending home activity sheets can be a useful tool for ensuring a good dialogue with parents and carers. Parents need to understand that the work is meant to be both fun and optional, and they need to be helped to have a clear understanding of how to approach the learning with their child.

## The Foundation Stage Curriculum

All the activities in this book are linked directly to the Foundation Stage curriculum as set out by the QCA in its document, *Curriculum guidance for the foundation stage*. Each activity is based on one of the Early Learning Goals for Knowledge and Understanding of the World. There are 60 differentiated versions of the activity sheets found on the CD-ROM, ensuring that a broad range of the Stepping Stones are also covered by the activities.

## The teacher's notes

To maximise the potential of the activity sheets, it is important to use them in conjunction with the accompanying teacher's notes. The notes will not only explain the main use for each sheet, but often they provide suggestions for introducing, differentiating and reinforcing the concept. For those sheets that have differentiated versions supplied on the CD-ROM there are brief notes explaining how the sheets have been adapted in order to support and extend learning.

## Using the photocopiable sheets

The photocopiable books are designed to be used in a number of ways. There may be suggestions to enlarge the sheet, and copy it on to card or coloured paper. You may also choose to laminate some of the sheets, particularly those that will be used as games or for visual stimuli to promote discussion.

Many of the photocopiable sheets may be used several times, as they have been written as open-ended tasks and can be reapplied with a new theme or subject matter. For example, some of the sheets are designed to be used in role-play settings and provide templates for the children to use.

When using photocopiable activity sheets with early years children it is important that the work is set within a context. Spend some time introducing and explaining the work and be on hand to guide and support the children as they complete or record the activity.

## The CD-ROM

The books in this series each have an accompanying CD-ROM containing the core activity sheets as featured in the book. These may be printed from your computer. In addition the CD-ROM contains an additional 60 activity sheets. These 60 printable sheets provide support and extension material for the 30 core activities that they are linked to, enabling practitioners to plan and provide differentiated material to suit a broad range of stages and abilities.

The CD-ROM should auto run when you insert it into your CD-ROM drive. For support in using the CD-ROM click on the 'Help' notes on the 'Main menu' screen.

# CHAPTER 1

# Let's play

**PAGE** 6
## Pattern allsorts

### Learning objective
Find out about and identify the uses of everyday technology and use information and communication technology and programmable toys to support their learning.

### What to do
Provide a selection of beads, buttons and sorting toys and make repeating patterns. Next, help the children to make a repeating pattern using a computer art program, by arranging Clip Art pictures on a page or using an interactive whiteboard to 'stamp' pictures in a pattern. Finish by completing the patterns on the photocopiable sheet.
**Support:** The most difficult pattern has been omitted.
**Extension:** The children are required to finish Jade's pattern and make a colour pattern too.

**PAGE** 7
## Weather centre

### Learning objective
Show an interest in ICT.

### What to do
Watch a weather forecast with the children. Comment on the technology involved – the computer generated maps and symbols, satellite images and so on. Set up a weather centre and let children use the tape recorder to record their own weather forecasts. Use the photocopiable sheet for the children to make their own weather diaries.
**Support:** Weather symbols are provided for the children to use.
**Extension:** Use a word processor for children to type out the days of the week and stick them onto the diary.

**PAGE** 8
## Invitation

### Learning objective
Perform simple functions on ICT apparatus.

### What to do
Work with pairs of children at a time to explore ways of sending cards and invitations using technology including e-card websites (such as www.foe.org.uk/cards/). Other ideas include printing digital photos or creating pictures using art and painting programs. Print off the children's work and then give each child a copy of the photocopiable sheet. Suggest that they plan an imaginary party for their toys in the home corner.

**PAGE** 9
## Shopping list
### Learning objective
Know how to operate simple equipment.

### What to do
Set up a shop role-play area with electronic toy tills with bar code scanners. Provide play food, packets, boxes and tins and encourage the children to take turns to be customers and shop assistants. Provide copies of the activity sheet and encourage the children to make lists, select their goods and then have them scanned and packed at the till.
**Support:** The list has been started to help younger children.
**Extension:** The children have to finish Bear's list as well as writing their own.

**PAGE** 10
## Play-writing
### Learning objective
Know how to operate simple equipment.

### What to do
Gather a collection of telephones together (real and toy) to explore. Model taking a phone message using the photocopiable sheet. Discuss what might be included on a menu. Set up your role-play area as a café and include a telephone for taking orders and messages. Place copies of the sheet in the area and encourage the children to use them in their play.

  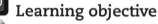 

**Support:** The menu has been started for the children and the message pad has been simplified.

**Extension:** A price column and lines have been added to the menu pad.

## Follow the tin robot
PAGE 11

### Learning objective
Find out about and identify the uses of everyday technology and use information and communication technology and programmable toys to support their learning.

### What to do
Provide a selection of mechanical and programmable toys for the children to explore. Discuss the mechanical features of robots and encourage the children to make up some robot movements. Give each child a copy of the photocopiable sheet. Invite them to colour the corresponding body part and tick the appropriate box when they have made their own body part move like a robot.

## Bubbles poem
PAGE 12

### Learning objective
Know how to operate simple equipment.

### What to do
Take a group of children outside and provide a range of bubble-blowing equipment, including bubble blowers and items such as battery-operated bubble machines. Let the children explore the equipment, pressing buttons and switches to control the flow. Back inside, provide an enlarged copy of the activity sheet and compose a bubble poem together as a group.

## Walkie-talkies
PAGE 13

### Learning objective
Perform simple functions on ICT apparatus.

### What to do
Demonstrate how to use walkie-talkies so that the children understand how to talk and receive messages. Allow two children at a time some free play with the equipment. After each pair has had their turn, provide a copy of the activity sheet and invite them to design their own pretend walkie-talkies.

**Support:** There are cut and stick badges provided for younger children to use.

**Extension:** Older children are additionally encouraged to make models of their walkie-talkie designs.

## Remote control
PAGE 14

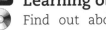

### Learning objective
Find out about and identify the uses of everyday technology and use information and communication technology and programmable toys to support their learning.

### What to do
Provide a remote-controlled vehicle and work with two or three children at a time. Help them to manipulate the controls to move the vehicle in a controlled fashion. Progress to setting challenges to direct the vehicle to a certain object. Next, provide the children with a copy of the photocopiable sheet and interpret the map together. Support the children as they take turns to direct the vehicle along the planned route.

**Support:** The map provided is simpler and easier to follow.

**Extension:** The children are additionally required to create their own map.

## Make yourself at home
PAGE 15

### Learning objective
Show an interest in ICT.

### What to do
Take small groups of children in turn on mini-house tours of your home corner. Ask them to spot any equipment that might be electrical (real or pretend). Talk about what they notice and relate it to any experiences they have from home. Now show the children an enlarged version of the photocopiable sheet. Talk about the picture and ask the children to point out and circle any electrical equipment that they notice.

# Pattern allsorts

This is Nathan's pattern.

He used beads.

This is Naima's pattern.

She used toy cars.

This is Jade's pattern.

She used buttons.

Draw your best pattern here.

EARLY YEARS
PHOTOCOPIABLES

SCHOLASTIC
www.scholastic.co.uk

# Weather centre

## My weather chart

| Monday | Tuesday | Wednesday | Thursday | Friday |
|--------|---------|-----------|----------|--------|
|        |         |           |          |        |

# Invitation

Dear _____

Please come to my party on

_____

_____

Love from _____

EARLY YEARS
PHOTOCOPIABLES

SCHOLASTIC
www.scholastic.co.uk

# Shopping list

Draw or write.

Bear's shopping list

_____

shopping list

# Play-writing

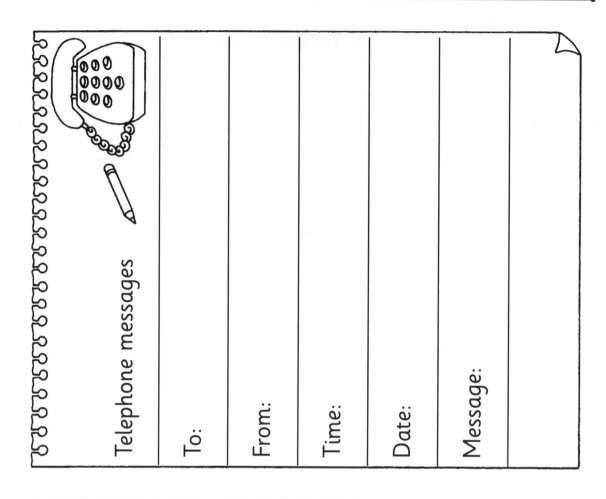

**Telephone messages**

To:

From:

Time:

Date:

Message:

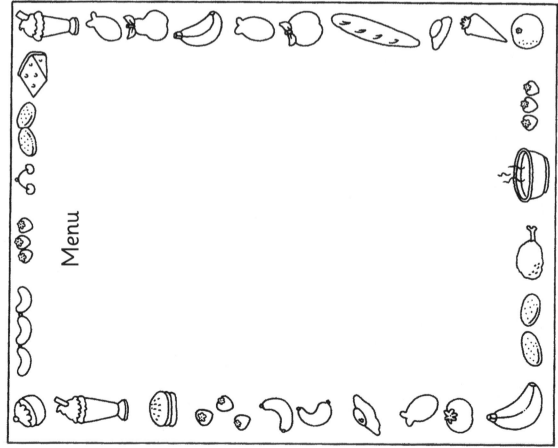

Menu

EARLY YEARS
PHOTOCOPIABLES

SCHOLASTIC
www.scholastic.co.uk

# Follow the tin robot

head ☐     body ☐     legs ☐

arms ☐     hands ☐     feet ☐

# Bubbles poem

Blow some bubbles. Write one word inside each bubble to describe what you see.

Bubbles, bubbles everywhere...

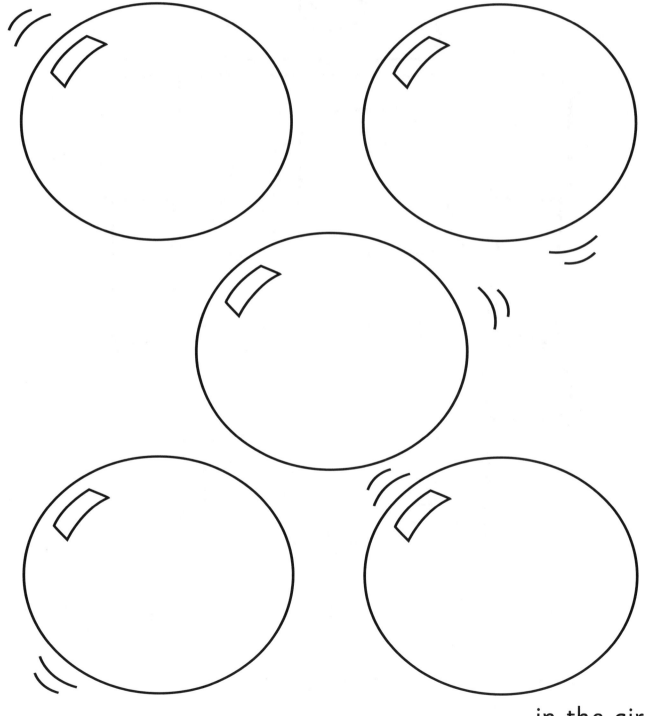

...in the air.

# Walkie-talkies

Design your own walkie-talkies.

# Remote control

Make your remote-controlled vehicle follow this route.

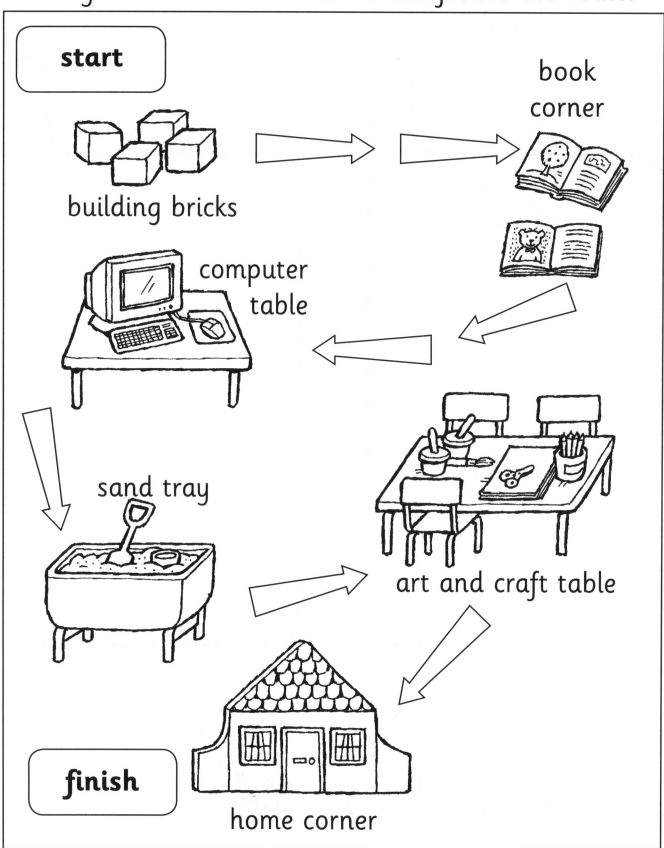

start

building bricks

book corner

computer table

sand tray

art and craft table

finish

home corner

EARLY YEARS
PHOTOCOPIABLES

■SCHOLASTIC
www.scholastic.co.uk

# Make yourself at home

Talk about the picture. Point out any electrical equipment.

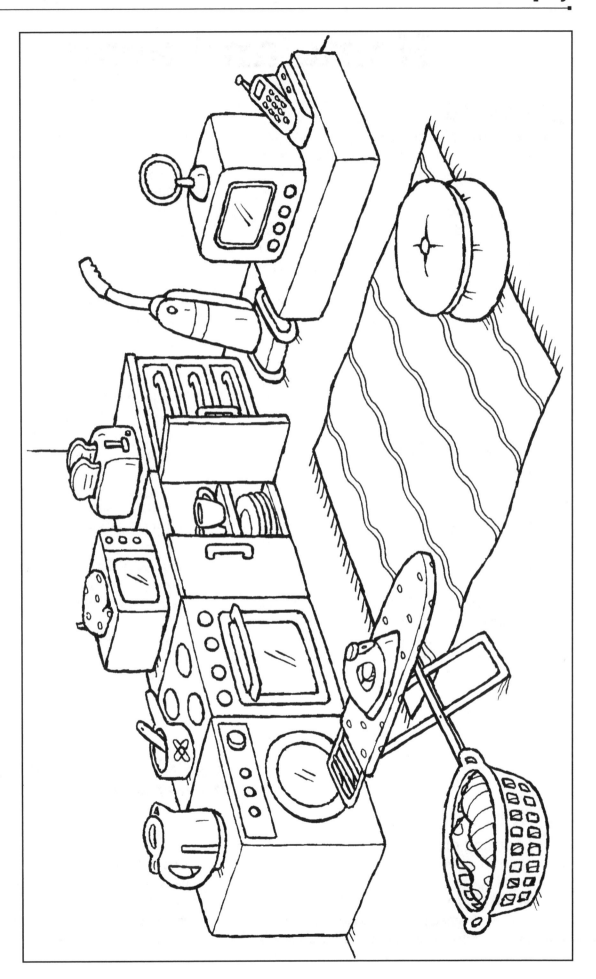

# CHAPTER 2

# Home and away

## PAGE 18 Cook it!

### Learning objective

 Find out about and identify the uses of everyday technology.

### What to do

Divide the children into groups each with an adult helper to make jelly (microwave), toast (toaster) and biscuits (cooker). When each child has had a turn, give them a copy of the activity sheet to draw the appliance that they used, and colour in the controls it had.

**Support:** Pictures are provided for the children to identify and colour in.

**Extension:** The children draw more detailed diagrams of the equipment used.

## PAGE 19 In the picture

### Learning objective

Perform simple functions on ICT apparatus.

### What to do

Make a banner for a wall display, 'A week in our setting' with captions such as 'In the morning' and 'Circle time'. Explain that you would like the children to take photographs of activities that occur every week at the setting. Show small groups of children at a time how to operate a camera, pointing out the viewfinder, lens and shutter button and how to review the pictures (digital cameras). Print photographs to add to the display. Provide the children with a copy of the activity sheet and invite them to colour it in and draw their favourite activity.

## PAGE 20 What do you hear?

### Learning objective

 Show an interest in ICT.

### What to do

Work with small groups and ask the children to name the objects shown and say what sort of noise each one makes. Can they try to

make a noise like any of the objects? Talk about whether the objects are mechanical, electrical or not and how they work.

**Support:** There are less objects for the children to discuss.

**Extension:** The children are challenged to draw two more electrical or mechanical objects that make a sound.

## PAGE 21 Photo fun!

### Learning objective

 Find out about and identify the uses of everyday technology.

### What to do

Take photographs of each child as they arrive at the group. Show them how you operate the equipment, if the camera is digital, show them how the images are stored and explain how you can delete and re-take any images. Talk about the pictures on the activity sheet and discuss the routines the children have. Ask them to cut out and sequence the pictures, sticking them onto a piece of paper. Next, give each child the photograph of themselves arriving at the group and add it to complete the sequence.

**Support:** Numbers and text have been added to simplify the activity for younger children.

**Extension:** Lines are provided for older children to attempt writing captions for the pictures.

## PAGE 22 Say the sound

### Learning objective

 Complete a simple program on the computer.

### What to do

Work with pairs of children and use the computer to play some card and matching games. Provide each child with a card copy of the sheet and ask them to sort the cards into pairs based on matching letter sounds. Let

them use Clip Art or an interactive whiteboard to create their own cards.

**Support:** The activity sheet provides just two letter sound pairs to match.

**Extension:** The children can use a computer to create a further two cards for the set.

## PAGE 23 When I went shopping
### Learning objective

Find out about and identify the uses of everyday technology.

### What to do

Enlarge a copy of the activity sheet and use it as the basis for a discussion about going shopping. Encourage the children to talk about their experiences. Focus on the whole process of going shopping, identify any technology that the children typically encounter, such as the use of a vehicle to get there, automatic doors, ticket machines, tills, bar code scanners and so on. Help the children to identify any places on the photocopiable sheet where technology may be used.

## PAGE 24 Yellow submarine
### Learning objective

Show an interest in ICT.

### What to do

Show the children some pictures or photographs of different types of boats and talk about how they move and float. Show them some pictures of submarines and talk about how these types of boat actually go right under the water. Enlarge a copy of the activity sheet and use the text for some related movement work. Give each child their own copy of the sheet and suggest that they colour it in once they have completed all the moves.

## PAGE 25 Staying safe

### Learning objective

Find out about and identify the uses of everyday technology.

### What to do

Enlarge a copy of the activity sheet and ask small groups of children if they can spot anything in the picture that they think is not safe. Talk about the dangers of electricity and electrical objects and help them to spot anything that uses electricity in the picture. Give each child their own copy of the activity sheet and ask them to colour in or circle the dangers that they see.

**Support:** The children are invited to talk about the dangers that have been circled.

**Extension:** In addition, the children are required to write some safety reminders.

## PAGE 26 There's a tiny caterpillar

### Learning objective

Find out about and identify the uses of everyday technology and use information and communication technology and programmable toys to support their learning.

### What to do

Use a CD-ROM or website with the children to find out about the life-cycle of a caterpillar (try a Google search). Provide each child with a copy of the activity sheet and ask them to cut out and sequence the pictures to make a zig-zag life-cycle book.

**Support:** There are only three pictures to sequence.

**Extension:** The children are required to add a picture to complete the sequence.

## PAGE 27 The lost puppy
### Learning objective

Use information and communication technology and programmable toys to support their learning.

### What to do

Enlarge the activity sheet to A3, stick it onto card and laminate it to make it more durable. Help the children to use a remote-controlled toy to act as the puppy. Navigate the toy along the map. Work with small groups and challenge each child to find a different way to take the puppy from 'Home' to the pond.

# Cook it!

I used the:

cooker                    microwave                    toaster

Did it have any of these?

- [ ] a door
- [ ] an on/off switch
- [ ] a timer
- [ ] a temperature switch
- [ ] a light
- [ ] numbers: 1 2 3 4 5 6 7 8 9

# In the picture

# What do you hear?

What sounds do these things make?

EARLY YEARS
PHOTOCOPIABLES

SCHOLASTIC
www.scholastic.co.uk

# Photo fun!

# Say the sound

# When I went shopping

# Yellow submarine

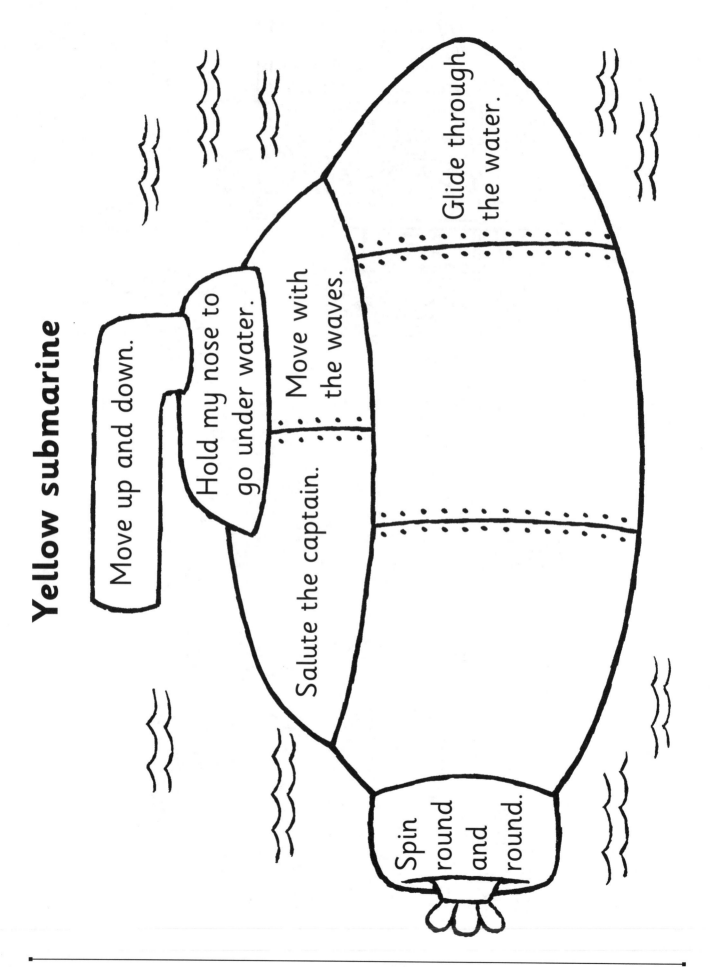

Move up and down.

Hold my nose to go under water.

Move with the waves.

Glide through the water.

Salute the captain.

Spin round and round.

EARLY YEARS
PHOTOCOPIABLES

SCHOLASTIC
www.scholastic.co.uk

# Staying safe

Colour in or circle the dangers that you can see in this picture.

# There's a tiny caterpillar

Colour in and cut out the pictures. Put them in order to make a zigzag book.

EARLY YEARS
PHOTOCOPIABLES

**SCHOLASTIC**
www.scholastic.co.uk

# The lost puppy

Draw lines to show how many different ways the puppy could walk home.

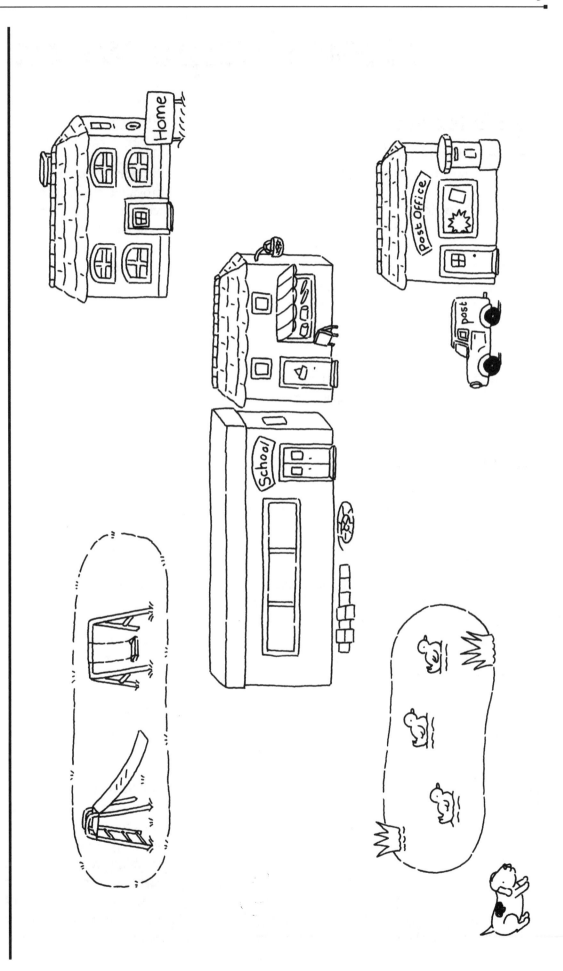

# CHAPTER 3

# How things work

## It's for you

### Learning objective

Know how to operate simple equipment.

### What to do

Make a display of a selection of telephones and invite the children to demonstrate how to use them to make and take calls. Talk together about what telephones are used for and how we make and receive calls. Give each child a copy of the photocopiable sheet. Ask them to look at the pictures of the people talking on the telephones. What do they think he/she is saying? Invite them to draw someone that they would like to speak to in the blank square.

## Write about...

### Learning objective

Complete a simple program on the computer.

### What to do

Work with pairs or individuals and show them how to switch on the computer, printer and monitor. Guide the children through some first steps in a word processing program such as using the keyboard using keys such as the space-bar, delete and shift keys. At later sessions help the children to change the font, size and colour. Record the children's progress on the photocopiable sheets.

## What's on TV?

### Learning objective

Know how to operate simple equipment.

### What to do

Bring a television into your setting and ask the children if they know how to use a remote control. Do they need to press any buttons? Let individuals demonstrate what they know. Give each child a copy of the activity sheet and invite them to draw a picture of their favourite programme on the screen and write about it underneath.

**Support:** A picture of a familiar rhyme is provided and the children are asked to guess what the picture is about.

**Extension:** The children are invited to draw and write about two of their favourite programmes.

## What's the difference?

### Learning objective

Find out about and identify the uses of everyday technology.

### What to do

Provide a selection of small-world vehicles for the children to examine and explore. Talk about their real counterparts, how they work and what makes them go. Ask the children to sort the toys to specified criteria, such as air, land and sea vehicles. Provide each child with an activity sheet and ask them to cut out and stick the pictures into two sets, explaining their reasons.

**Support:** There are less pictures to sort, and the rings have been labelled.

**Extension:** The children are required to sort some pictures into three categories.

## Pairs

### Learning objective

Perform simple functions on ICT apparatus.

### What to do

If possible provide access to a real washing machine. Alternatively provide pictures of washing machines and a toy washing machine that has buttons and switches. Together, consider what a washing machine does. Talk about the different programmes and cycles and look at the buttons, dials and switches. Wash (or pretend to wash) a big load of socks! Enlist the children's help to sort them into pairs. Provide each child with a copy of the activity sheet and ask them to cut out and stick the pairs on the line, counting in twos as they do so.

**Support:** The children are simply required to match the sock pairs and stick them on the line.

**Extension:** The children are required to add extra socks to make 16 in total.

PAGE 35 # Heavier or lighter?

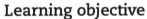

## Learning objective
Know how to operate simple equipment.

## What to do
Provide a range of scales including some electronic scales. Invite the children to measure a random assortment of objects including some potatoes. Provide each child with an activity sheet and ask them to choose a potato and weigh it and then compare it to some other objects, sorting them into heavier or lighter than a potato.

**Support:** The children are asked to weigh specific things and may cut out and sort the pictures provided, adding pictures that are heavier than a potato to the circle.

**Extension:** The children keep a table of results.

PAGE 36 # Play time!

## Learning objective
Know how to operate simple equipment.

## What to do
Provide a collection of types of clock including digital, mechanical, alarm, watches and so on. Ideally provide one that the children can disassemble to look at the cogs and wheels and so on. Print the activity sheet onto card and cut into individual cards. Work with groups and challenge individuals to pick out cards and help them to show the times on one of the clocks.

**Support:** Cards to 6 o'clock only have been provided.

**Extension:** The cards also show some half-past times.

PAGE 37 # Helping hands

## Learning objective
Show an interest in ICT.

## What to do
Explain that you are going to take photographs of the children being kind. Discuss how a camera works and whether it uses film or is a digital camera. At the end of the session ask the children to consider what their hands have been doing. Give each child a copy of the sheet and ask them to fill the box with a photograph of themselves being helpful.

PAGE 38 # Our soup recipe

## Learning objective
Show an interest in ICT.

## What to do
Choose a simple soup recipe, discuss the ingredients and show the children some mixing and blending equipment. Talk about the difference between a manual whisk and an electric blender. As you make some soup let the children, under careful supervision, push the button on a blender or liquidiser to puree the vegetables. Provide each child with an activity sheet and help them to write out the main ingredients they used.

**Support:** The children draw the ingredients.

**Extension:** The children are also invited to write how the soup was made.

PAGE 39 # Water search

## Learning objective
Find out about and identify the uses of everyday technology and use information and communication technology and programmable toys to support their learning.

## What to do
Enlarge a copy of the activity sheet and talk about it with groups of children. Invite them to complete it and describe how the equipment in each room works. Can they tell you which objects are powered by electricity? What other objects might go in the rooms?

# It's for you!

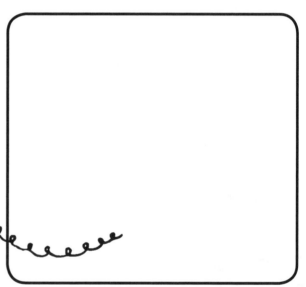

EARLY YEARS
PHOTOCOPIABLES

SCHOLASTIC
www.scholastic.co.uk

# Write about...

| I can... | by myself | with help |
|---|---|---|
| write some letters | | |
| write some numbers | | |
| find the letters of my name on the keyboard | | |
| find and use the space bar | | |
| find and use the delete key | | |
| make small and big letters | | |
| change the font | | |
| change the colour of the text | | |
| change the size of the text | | |
| save my work | | |
| print out my work | | |

# What's on TV?

# What's the difference?

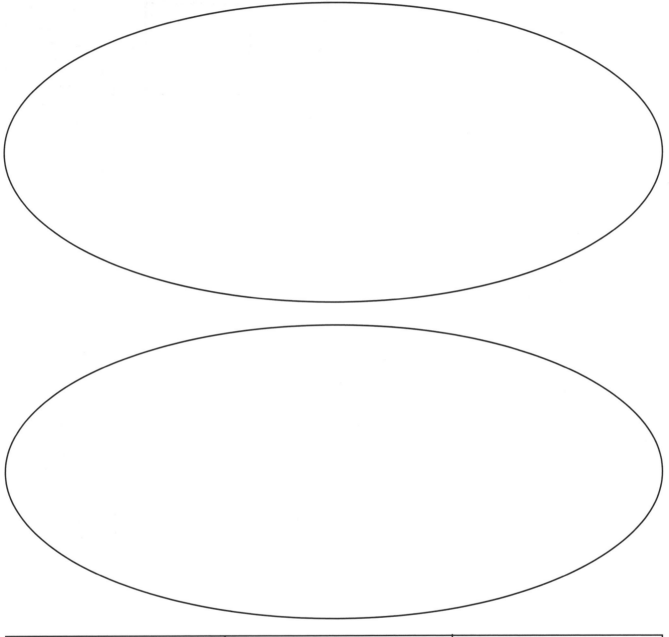

EARLY YEARS
PHOTOCOPIABLES

ICT 33

# Pairs

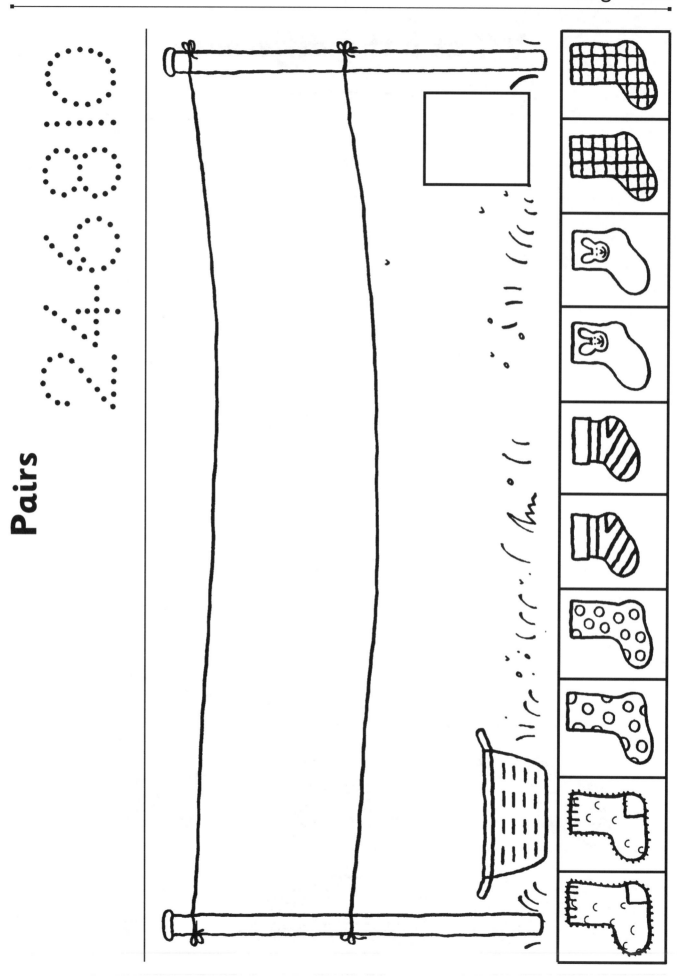

# Heavier or lighter?

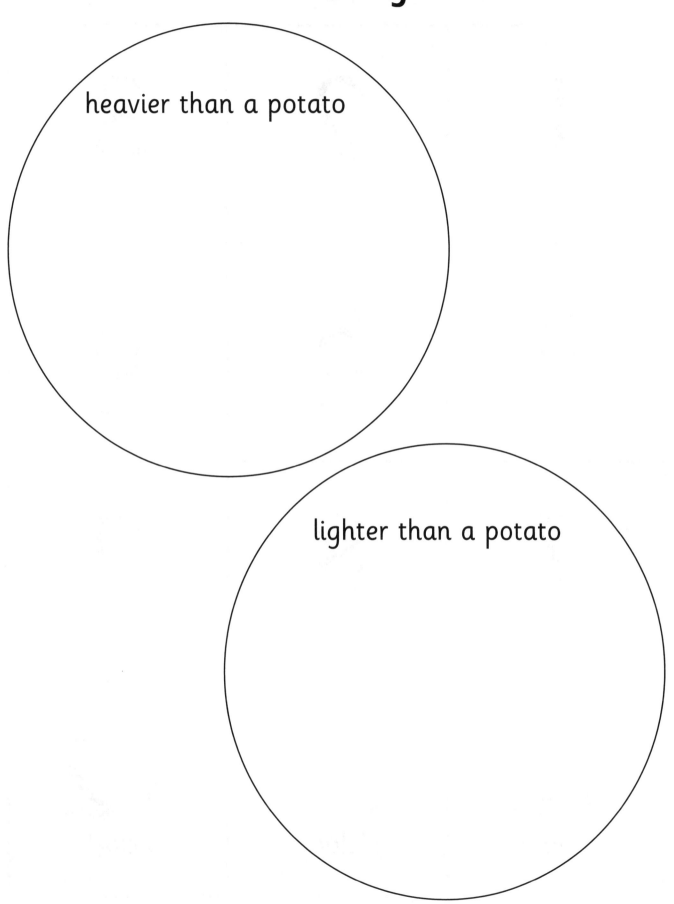

heavier than a potato

lighter than a potato

EARLY YEARS
PHOTOCOPIABLES

# Play time!

| | | |
|---|---|---|
| **1**<br>o'clock | **2**<br>o'clock | **3**<br>o'clock |
| **4**<br>o'clock | **5**<br>o'clock | **6**<br>o'clock |
| **7**<br>o'clock | **8**<br>o'clock | **9**<br>o'clock |
| **10**<br>o'clock | **11**<br>o'clock | **12**<br>o'clock |

EARLY YEARS
PHOTOCOPIABLES

SCHOLASTIC
www.scholastic.co.uk

# Helping hands

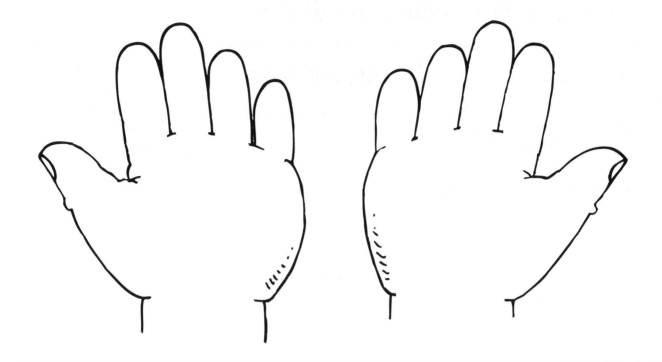

Name _____

# Our soup recipe

Draw and write your ingredients.

Vegetable soup

We used:

water

# Water search

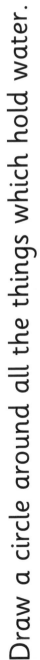

Draw a circle around all the things which hold water.

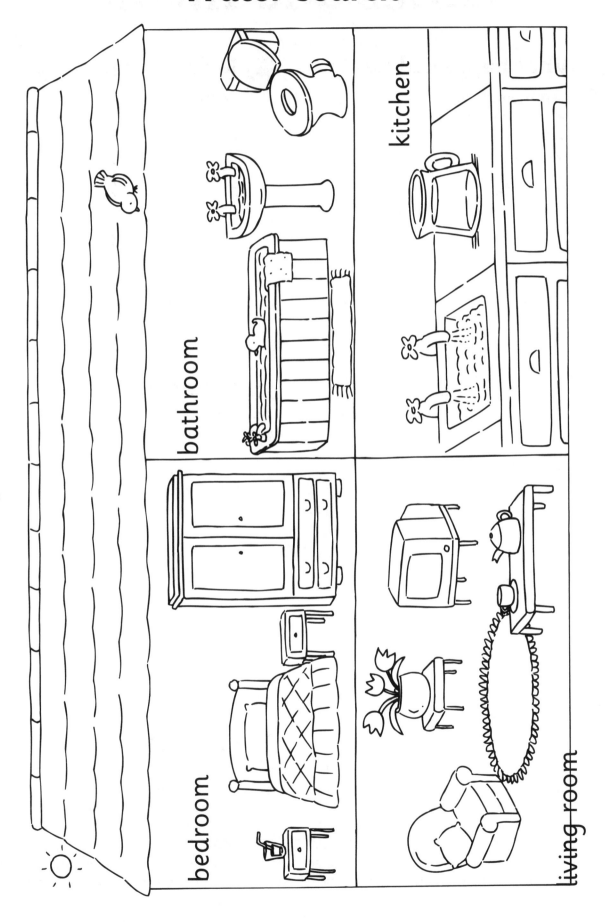

kitchen

bathroom

bedroom

living room

# CHAPTER 4

# Stories and rhymes

## What happened next?

### Learning objective
Use information and communication technology and programmable toys to support their learning.

### What to do
Provide a selection of books with a version of 'Goldilocks and the Three Bears'. Draw the children's attention to any differences in the way the story is retold. Explain to the children that you will work with two children at a time and be their writer, using a word processor to write the children's own versions of the story. Print off the children's stories and encourage them to illustrate the pages, to make their own book versions. Finally give each child a copy of the activity sheet and ask them to draw an alternative ending for the story.

**Support:** Two pictures focus on two incidents in the story. There is space for the adult to scribe the children's 'stories'.

**Extension:** The children are challenged to draw two pictures to illustrate the beginning and ending of the story.

## Story time

### Learning objective
Complete a simple program on the computer.

### What to do
Choose a favourite CD-ROM story and show it to a small group of children at a time. Explain what you are doing at each stage. Look at all the options on the screen and choose 'Read to me' (or similar) and enjoy the story together. Make named copies of the activity sheet and place them in a file next to the computer. Next, work with small groups of children at a time and enjoy browsing through the CD-ROM together. Encourage them to manipulate the 'pages' and make a note of their ability to do so independently.

## Make up the story

### Learning objective
Complete a simple program on the computer.

### What to do
Enlarge a copy of the activity sheet and ask a small group of children to talk about the dragon picture with you. Ask: Who do you think the child might be? Where has the dragon come from? Where is it going to? Write down the children's ideas and invite them to work with a partner and take turns to use a drawing program on the computer to create pictures to go with their stories.

## Super stories

### Learning objective
Show an interest in ICT.

### What to do
Talk about the children's favourite traditional stories, encouraging them to tell you why they like them. Remind them that stories may also be enjoyed on cassettes, CDs, as part of television programmes, on CD-ROMs, Leap pads and so on. Work with a child at a time to fill out the details on the photocopiable sheet, scribing where appropriate.

**Support:** The children are encouraged to draw a picture about their chosen story.

**Extension:** In addition the children are asked to write about other stories that they like.

 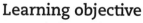
## Favourite books

### Learning objective
Use information and communication technology to support their learning.

### What to do
Enjoy a selection of stories in different formats across the course of a week. Set up a listening area with some new books on

cassettes and CDs. Talk about the children's favourites. Provide the children with the activity sheet and ask them to write down books that they have enjoyed listening to.

**Support:** The children draw pictures and an adult can help by scribing their responses.

**Extension:** The children are also asked to say why they enjoyed their chosen books.

## Tell a tale
PAGE 47

### Learning objective
Use information and communication technology and programmable toys to support their learning.

### What to do
Tell the children the story of 'Goldilocks and the Three Bears', encouraging them to join in with the refrains. Give each child a copy of the photocopiable sheet and ask them to colour, cut out and stick the pictures on paper in the correct order. Leave space beneath each picture to add some words. Work with individual children and help them to use a word processing program to write words to go with each picture. Stick the children's words underneath the matching pictures.

## Hickory Dickory Dock
PAGE 48

### Learning objective
Show an interest in ICT.

### What to do
Provide each child with a copy of the photocopiable sheet, ask them to colour in the pictures, cut along the lines and stick the clock onto strong card, punching a hole where indicated. Stick the mice back to back and attach them to a length of wool or string. Thread the wool through the hole in the clock and tie a knot in the other end. Pull the knot to make the mouse run up the clock, let go and the mouse will run down.

## Talking books
PAGE 49

### Learning objective
Know how to operate simple equipment.

### What to do
Find out what the children understand by the term 'Talking books'. Show them some examples from around your setting. Discuss the activity and questions on the photocopiable sheet.

**Support:** The children are required to draw arrows to match pieces of equipment.

**Extension:** The children make a list of the materials that they will use to make their talking book machine.

## Plug in and listen
PAGE 50

### Learning objective
Perform simple functions on ICT apparatus.

### What to do
Work with small groups of children. Ask them what story the pictures on the photocopiable sheet show. Tell the story together, asking the children to join in with any repetitive phrases. Put the children into pairs and provide puppets to help with their storytelling. Show them how to use a simple cassette recorder to record their voices. Allocate a picture to each pair and ask them to practise saying their part of the story. Help the children to record their section. Play back the finished story.

**Support:** Just three pictures are provided.

**Extension:** The children are encouraged to plan their story, adding notes under each picture.

## CD favourites
PAGE 51

### Learning objective
Show an interest in ICT.

### What to do
Talk about favourite CD-ROM stories together. Show an enlarged copy of the activity sheet to the children and explain that you would like them to decide which pictures go together. Give each child their own copy of the sheet and ask them to draw lines to match the pictures to the CD-ROMs.

**Support:** There are only two sets to match.

**Extension:** There are blank spaces for the children to add their own illustrations.

# What happened next?

# Story time

| I can... | by myself | with help |
|---|---|---|
| choose 'Read to me' | | |
| choose 'Play inside the story' | | |
| find the pointer on screen | | |
| move the mouse | | |
| point to the | | |
| point to the | | |
| move to the next page | | |
| move to the previous page | | |
| print out my favourite page | | |
| Comments | | |

# Make up the story

Talk about what you can see.
Make up your own story.

EARLY YEARS
PHOTOCOPIABLES

# Super stories

My name is _____

Title of book _____

_____

I liked it because _____

_____

_____

It tells the story of _____

_____

_____

EARLY YEARS
PHOTOCOPIABLES

# Favourite books

My name is _____

I have read

1 _____

_____

2 _____

_____

3 _____

_____

4 _____

_____

# Tell a tale

# Hickory Dickory Dock

Colour in and cut out the pictures.

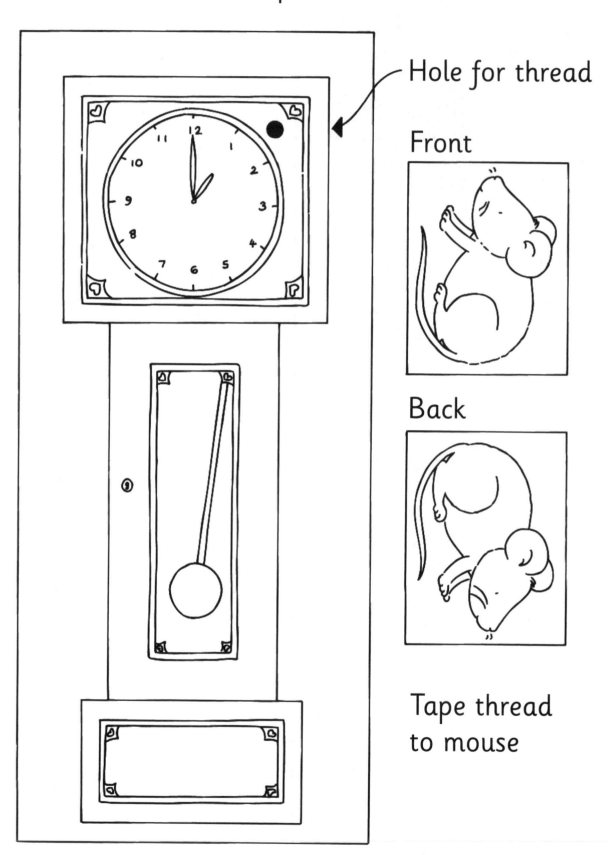

Hole for thread

Front

Back

Tape thread
to mouse

EARLY YEARS
PHOTOCOPIABLES

■SCHOLASTIC
www.scholastic.co.uk

# Talking books

Invent a talking book machine.

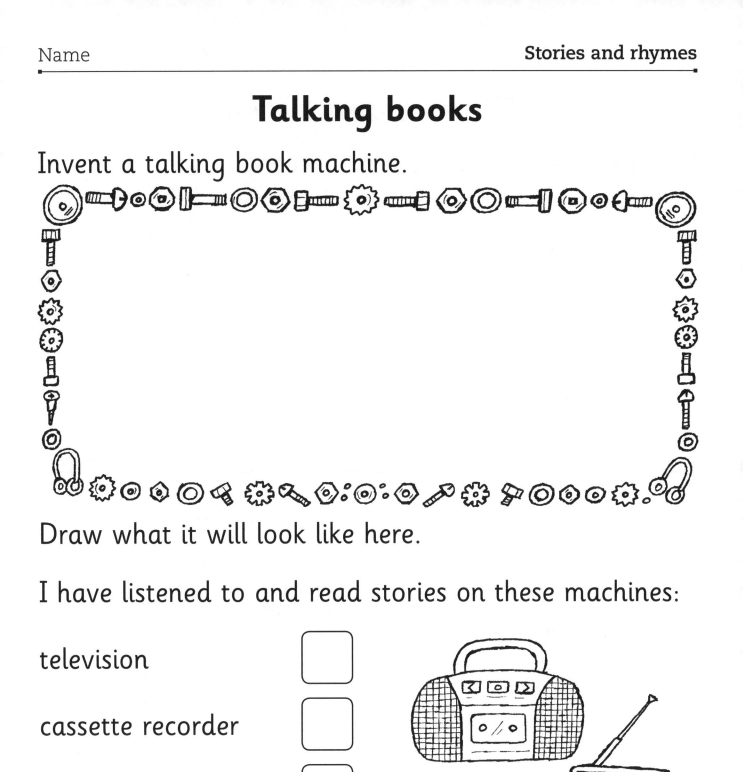

Draw what it will look like here.

I have listened to and read stories on these machines:

television ☐

cassette recorder ☐

radio ☐

CD player ☐

Leap pad ☐

computer CD-ROM ☐

# Plug in and listen

Use these pictures to retell and record a story.

EARLY YEARS
PHOTOCOPIABLES

■SCHOLASTIC
www.scholastic.co.uk

# CD favourites

Draw lines to match the pictures to the CD-ROMs.

# Creative fun

## Art gallery

### Learning objective

Complete a simple program on the computer.

### What to do

Set up an art gallery by displaying art prints and posters and signs such as 'Art exhibition' and 'To the gallery'. Prepare some card frames for the children's work. Help the children to work individually on the computer to use an art program to create a picture for the gallery. Show them how to print and frame their work. Provide copies of the activity sheet and ask them to complete the pictures and draw one of their own.

**Support:** The children have to finish one picture and create one of their own.

**Extension:** The children are required to finish two pictures and draw two of their own.

## The writing corner

### Learning objective

Show an interest in ICT.

### What to do

Talk together about the different ways that we can write including using word processors, computers and hand-held computers. Consider all the ways that we can send and receive letters (through the post, via email, faxes and so on). Provide each child with a card copy of the activity sheet and ask the children to draw a picture on one side and help them to fill in their address and write a message on the back.

**Support:** Some words have been supplied.

**Extension:** The children may also design their own stamp.

## Musical interlude

### Learning objective

Perform simple functions on ICT apparatus.

### What to do

Provide an electronic keyboard and work with two or three children at a time to experiment with the different sounds it can make. Identify how to create the sound of a drum, violin, piano and other instruments. Next, provide each child with a copy of the activity sheet and invite the children to use some junk materials to create a 'music box'. They can then stick the circles on to their box as pretend buttons. Allow them some free play with their music boxes and provide percussion instruments too.

## Sandcastle flags

### Learning objective

Complete a simple program on the computer.

### What to do

Show the children a CD-ROM atlas or a website that shows flags. Work with pairs of children at a time and talk together about the colours, patterns and symbols that they notice on the flags. Let the children experiment with an art program on the computer to design and decorate their own flags. Provide each child with a copy of the photocopiable page and ask them to talk about and colour the flags.

**Support:** Only the two most simple flags are provided.

**Extension:** The children are also invited to design a flag of their own.

## Decorating

### Learning objective

Complete a simple program on the computer.

### What to do

Work with two children at a time and use an art program on the computer to experiment with colours, patterns and textures. Provide

each child with a copy of the photocopiable sheet and ask them to create pieces of wallpaper and carpet to decorate the room. Invite them to take turns to create some designs to print out and stick to fit the space on the sheet.

PAGE 59

## Little red book

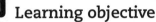

### Learning objective

Use information and communication technology to support their learning.

### What to do

Give each child a copy of the photocopiable sheet and demonstrate how to cut and fold it to make a small book. Invite the children to take a turn to use the computer to draw or find Clip Art images of other red objects and to type the words underneath. Help them to print out their pictures, and stick them in the blank pages to complete their books.

**Support:** Four pictures are provided.

**Extension:** The children are also required to write the words to go with the pictures.

PAGE 60

## The paint shop

### Learning objective

Use information and communication technology to support their learning.

### What to do

Use a CD-ROM or paint program to practise some colour mixing using the computer. Let the children work with a partner and encourage them to discuss their findings. Invite the children to use a copy of the photocopiable sheet and some real paints to record their findings.

PAGE 61

## At the park

### Learning objective

Use information and communication technology to support their learning.

### What to do

Scan a copy of the activity sheet onto your computer and if available, display the picture on your interactive whiteboard (or alternatively, enlarge it and show it to the children). Talk about the picture and together identify all the things that begin with the letter 'p'.

**Support:** The children are simply encouraged to talk about the picture.

**Extension:** The children are invited to write the 'p' words in the spaces provided.

PAGE 62

## Musical maps

### Learning objective

Use programmable toys to support their learning.

### What to do

Using the sheet as a guide, draw a series of boxes and arrows onto a giant piece of sugar paper. Ask the children to sit around the edges of the 'map'. Provide a programmable toy such as a Roamer and help the children to guide it along the map. Discuss the musical symbols on the photocopiable sheet, draw some on pieces of paper and place them on the large map. Ask the children to direct the Roamer to each box and invite a child to play the corresponding instrument as it reaches a new destination. Finally let the children create and play their own musical maps using the photocopiable sheet.

**Support:** The children are asked to make a simple three picture music map.

**Extension:** The children are required to draw three symbols of their own.

PAGE 63

## Christmas stamps

### Learning objective

Perform simple functions on ICT apparatus.

### What to do

Show the children the photocopiable sheet and ask each child to design a Christmas stamp. Tell the children that they may use the digital camera to take some Christmassy images which can be downloaded and printed. Alternatively they may use Clip Art or art programs on the computer to create a festive scene.

# Art gallery

SCHOLASTIC
www.scholastic.co.uk

# The writing corner

# Musical interlude

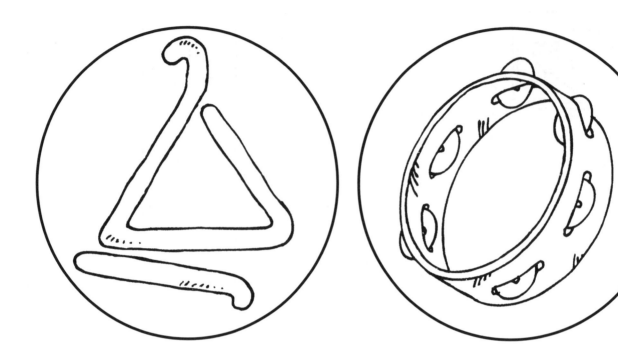

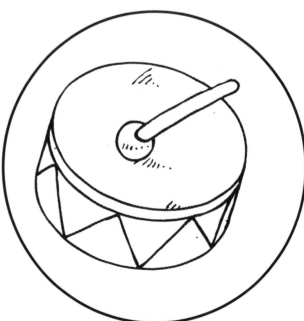

# Sandcastle flags

Colour in and cut out these flags.

# Decorating

Use printing materials to decorate this room.
Add fabric curtains and carpet.

EARLY YEARS
PHOTOCOPIABLES

SCHOLASTIC
www.scholastic.co.uk

# Little red book

Cut out, colour and fold to make a book. Draw red things in your book.

post box

Fold

tomato

# The paint shop

Record your paint mixing work here.
I used these colours:

paint chart

# At the park

Find the things beginning with 'p'.

# Musical maps

Make your own tune! Colour in the pictures. Cut them out and stick them on a square. Play the music.

START

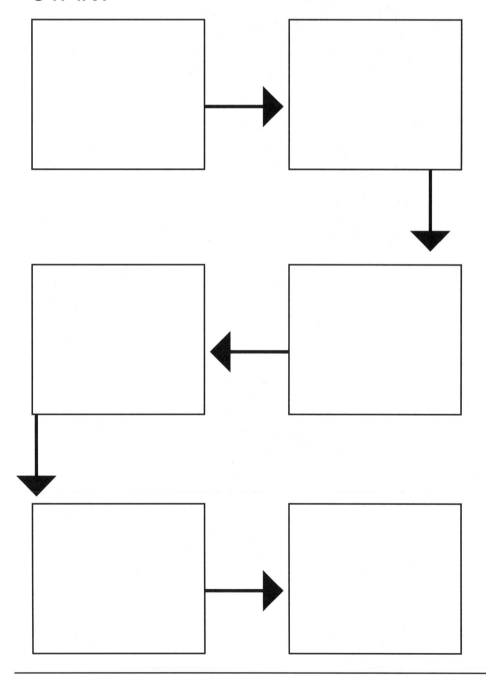

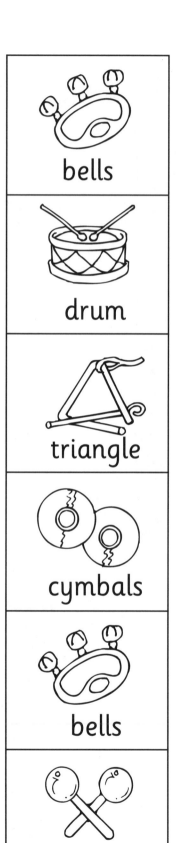

bells

drum

triangle

cymbals

bells

shakers

EARLY YEARS
PHOTOCOPIABLES

SCHOLASTIC
www.scholastic.co.uk

# Christmas stamps

**SCHOLASTIC**
www.scholastic.co.uk

EARLY YEARS
PHOTOCOPIABLES

## In this series:

ISBN 0-439-96545-4
ISBN 978-0439-96545-3

ISBN 0-439-96546-2
ISBN 978-0439-96546-0

ISBN 0-439-96547-0
ISBN 978-0439-96547-7

ISBN 0-439-994488-0
ISBN 978-0439-94488-5

ISBN 0-439-94489-9
ISBN 978-0439-94489-2

To find out more, call: 0845 603 9091
or visit our website www.scholastic.co.uk